The Radiance of Her Face

*A Triptych in Honor of
Mary Immaculate*

The
RADIANCE
of
HER FACE

*A Triptych in Honor of
Mary Immaculate*

⊕

Dom Xavier Perrin, O.S.B.
Abbot of Quarr Abbey

First published
by Second Spring, 2017
www.secondspring.co.uk
an imprint of Angelico Press
© Dom Xavier Perrin, O.S.B. 2017
Foreword © Dom Benedict Hardy, O.S.B. 2017

The Radiance of Her Face is an enlarged version of *Regards sur l'Immaculée* (Editions du Carmel, 2006). The book has been translated by Sr Lætitia Payne of St Cecilia's Abbey, Ryde, Isle of Wight, in collaboration with Sr Deirdre Michael Clarke of the Ordinariate Sisters of the Blessed Virgin Mary, Kingstanding, Birmingham. It has also been translated into Swedish as *Vad du är skön Maria* (Gaudete, 2013).

For information, address:
Angelico Press
4709 Briar Knoll Dr.
Kettering, OH 45429
angelicopress.com

978-1-62138-306-2 (pbk)
978-1-62138-307-9 (cloth)
978-1-62138-308-6 (ebook)

Cover image: Modified from *Immaculate Conception*, attributed to Diego Velázquez or Alonso Cano, between 1618 and 1620.
Cover design: Michael Schrauzer

In Honor of Mary Immaculate

CONTENTS

Foreword

THE LONG AWAITED PUBLICATION IN ENGLISH translation of Père Xavier's little work on Mary Immaculate is an event very much to be welcomed. The original was first published in French in 2006. Many who were lucky enough to read it then have longed that it be made available to the English-speaking world. Happily, the intervening years have allowed the author to add two chapters, now seeing the light for the first time.

There are many books about Our Lady, but I know of none that can compare with this. Here we find ourselves privileged participants in a contemplative gaze. The French title, so difficult to render adequately in English, refers to this gaze: *Regards sur l'Immaculée*. It is a gaze both steady and serene, a gaze full of love and wonder, informed by faith and rooted in scholarly knowledge of the Scriptures and the Tradition of the Catholic Church. While the author never once speaks of himself, we cannot fail to sense how profoundly personal is this gaze. The text is full of interesting information, yet above all flows from a heart aflame with love for Mary Immaculate. And it is marked, inevitably, by the training and tradition of the author. He writes as a Benedictine monk of the Solesmes Congregation, from Brittany in France; as one whose life is given up to the worship of God, especially in the solemn liturgy; as a lover of art and music, especially sacred art and Gregorian Chant; as a theologian, and a contemplative; as one whose instinct is to stay quietly out of the limelight, but also as one who has something important to say; above all, as one whose life has been touched by a vision of radiant beauty.

Those who already rejoice in fervent devotion to Mary will find their love for her here nourished, stirred, refreshed, confirmed, given new impetus. But perhaps for many the mystery of the Immaculate Conception remains somewhat abstract, remote, inaccessible: doubtless well-formulated theologically, its truth guaranteed by the Church, but not so very relevant in the daily life of faith. If such there be, Père Xavier's book will open up to them a new vista of understanding: for he shows how this mystery has an essential place in the history of salvation, in the life of the Church, and in our own Christian and human lives. Perhaps also this book might fall into the hands of some who hitherto have lacked the confidence to turn to Mary, who feel they do not really understand how we can pray to her, or relate to her, or love her. Surely for such these pages could be truly liberating, even life-giving; offering access to a new dimension of the Christian life; inviting entry into a prayer that is deeper, more confident, more free, more effective.

Yes, it is true that there are some rather bold statements to be found here. Anyone entirely committed to the cause of the sixteenth-century Reformers will scarcely find them easy to swallow. Yet there is nothing here of controversy, polemics, or antagonism to anyone or anything. Nor as a matter of fact is there any exaggeration or excess. What is taught here can withstand the most rigorous theological scrutiny—it is simply an unfolding of one of the truths of our faith.

"Turning our eyes to Mary Immaculate," according to the excellent subtitle given by the English translators, we find ourselves crying out, with the Swedish translators of the original title: *Vad du är skön Maria!*—"How beautiful you are, Mary!"

A contemplative gaze at Mary Immaculate has the power to change us, to convert us, to soften our hard hearts, to open us up to the transforming power of the Holy Spirit, to help us renounce all resistance to Christ's redemptive work, so that it may have its full effect in us as it did in her.

Here then is a book to be savored, to be read slowly and repeatedly, to be passed on to others. May it be a blessing for all who encounter it, and may it help us all identify ourselves wholly with the Blessed Virgin, who magnified the Lord with the whole of her being in gratitude and joy, and who teaches us to do the same.

Dom Benedict Hardy OSB
Prior of Pluscarden Abbey
22 August 2017, Feast of the Queenship of Mary

Introduction

"I do not know how to put into words what I experienced, what I saw:
the beauty and the brightness, the radiance. . . ."
— Saint Catherine Labouré

"She had blue eyes. . . ."
— Saint Bernadette Soubirous

THERE IS NOTHING AS BEAUTIFUL AS THE BLESSED Virgin's smile. How could the one who was "full of grace" not be radiant with beauty? If we are not all called, like Saint Catherine Labouré or Saint Bernadette, to see the Blessed Virgin with our bodily eyes, we all long to have her beauty revealed to us.

The longing to gaze upon the Immaculate Virgin is not a matter of superficial devotion, of being greedy for sensible consolations, but rather a genuine requirement of Christian contemplation. Faith, which knows how to believe without seeing, nevertheless contains within itself a thirst for sight which shall only be satisfied in heaven, but which even now orients our gaze towards eternal beauty.

By meditation on the Word of God, in the school of the Church's Magisterium, of the teaching of the Saints, and of that right feeling for the truths of the faith which we call the *sensus fidelium*—that understanding of the faith found within the people of God and transmitted in the monuments of living tradition—the eye of faith can discover with wonder the light that radiates from the face of the Immaculate Virgin.

The Iconographic tradition of both East and West has loved to represent Saint Luke painting the Virgin. This symbolism signifies the Marian privilege of the Evangelist, who has devoted more of his narrative than any of the other Evangelists to the things concerning the Mother of Our Savior. Yet it also suggests a universal message, for every believer who exposes himself or herself in prayer to the Light of the Spirit is invited in a similar way to paint in his or her own soul the face of the Immaculate Virgin, a pure reflection of the "Glory of God in the face of Christ" (2 Cor. 4:6).

> Of you has my heart said: "Seek his face."
> It is your face, Lord, that I seek;
> do not hide your face from me. (Ps. 27:8–9)

Abbaye Sainte-Anne de Kergonan, 8 December 2005

I

A Triptych in Honor
of Mary Immaculate

WE ARE ALL FAMILIAR WITH THOSE FLEMISH
paintings which depict variations on a theme
upon the hinged panels of an altar piece. Let
us imitate them and set up a triptych. First of all we shall
look at the two side panels, keeping the centre one, the
most important one, till last. These three panels will be
like three meditations on the Immaculate Conception, in
order to teach us to look at and love her as God sees and
loves her, in order to enter upon the life-giving contemplation of this mystery of beauty and love.

The Young Woman and the Angel

The first panel—consider it on the right or the left, as
you wish—depicts the announcement being made to
Mary. In his account of the Annunciation, Saint Luke has
given us the starting point for every Marian meditation. If
we wish to contemplate more especially the mystery of
the Immaculate Conception, we can return once again in
spirit to Nazareth. The dialogue, which is so full of meaning, between the young girl and the angel, between Gab-
riel and Mary, can resonate in us anew.

7

The scene takes place in Elizabeth's sixth month. A woman is expecting a child. And because this elderly woman is here expecting her first child, because her husband, the priest Zechariah, had this birth announced to him in a vision during his service in the temple at Jerusalem, this pregnancy is particularly heavy with meaning. This woman symbolizes an entire epoch, the period of waiting, of straining towards something new that will be both fruit and gift. Ever since Sarah, Abraham's wife, expecting Isaac, the son of the promise, the cycle of generations has been orientated towards a future which God Himself had guaranteed. Humanity recognises its own destiny in these women who were waiting for the Child God Himself would give.

Upon this backdrop of hope, appears Mary. When the angel visits her, she is a young girl, "a virgin, betrothed to a man named Joseph, of the house of David." Nothing seems to distinguish her from other young girls, from other fiancées in this little town of Nazareth. Nevertheless, it is indeed to her that the angel is sent, and it is her that he greets with the almost unheard-of title: "full of grace," in Greek *kecharitomene*. It signifies, at one and the same time, one who has been filled with grace and one who will remain so.

The angel contemplates Mary, full of grace. She represents fullness itself. God has rested His favor and His good pleasure upon her. He has made her the privileged object of His love. He has filled her with all the effects of His tender mercy. And, in Mary, that is essential. This fullness is not simply an ornament, a covering or rich robe that one might place upon a very modest stand. It is what she is in her deepest self. In perfect simplicity, her very being exists caught up by grace in a way innate to her, sanctified, divinized. She is infinitely magnified in the original nuptials of a created participation in the divine nature. This ennobles her to the highest degree and lifts her to an outstanding level of purity, goodness and beauty. Never has a creature corresponded so perfectly to the Creator's vision of beauty. Never has a woman been so thoroughly a woman according to the heart of God. Never has grace, the divine good pleasure, been so fully poured forth into a creature.

The angel, who habitually contemplates the face of God, immediately recognizes in Mary an outstanding resemblance to the One Who created them both. Is he, perhaps, taken aback, astonished to encounter among men a person so divine? Yet the most astonished one is Mary herself. She is troubled, greatly troubled, and, says the text: "she considered in her mind what sort of greeting this might be."

On the one hand, thoroughly immersed in God, she is unaware of herself. On the other, she senses that God is about to make known to her his astonishing will.

Unaware of herself—she is hidden from her own eyes. Fully human and royally divine, she is a vessel full of tender mercy, and it is with tender mercy that she looks upon those who surround her. This mercy, received from the Father, makes her infinitely humble, perfectly compassionate. She is entirely at the service of her neighbor, incapable of comparing herself with others, for she is totally incapable of turning in upon herself. She is completely humble, for she is always perfectly placed, with regard to God, in free, glad and total dependence on Him. She is so humble that people do not notice her, do not offer her any compliments, do not think anything of her or look at her. She possesses something of God's own invisibility, which is the invisibility of Love in its pure state, inaccessible to the creature unless God lifts it up and transforms it in order to make it capable of loving as God loves, of knowing as He knows, of participating in His transcendent purity. Perhaps it is the first time that anyone greets her, calls her by her name, that she is noticed, looked at or pointed out.

Then it is that Mary is deeply troubled. She does not stop for a moment to look at herself. She only understands that the fullness of grace which she has enjoyed until now without knowing the reason for it, is about to be given all its meaning. She knows that she has been consecrated by God, and she herself has responded to His divine attention by consecrating herself entirely to the One from Whom she has received everything. The time has come for her to learn the mission for which God has destined her.

She is startled and perhaps even very deeply disturbed.

The angel is going to tell her in a few words, heavy with all the resonances of the biblical Word, the role that is now entrusted to her. To be the mother of a son, who will be called Jesus—which means *savior*—who will be great, the son of the Most High, heir of David, one who is to inherit a kingdom that will have no end: all that she sensed, all that she foresaw in the angel's greeting now becomes clear and precise in her heart. She will be the mother of the Messiah, of the Son of David, the Savior of the world. All that she is, she is for him, in view of him, and in a certain sense, thanks to him, in dependence upon him. For he could not possibly come "from below," from her and from a man from here below. Mary, then, by her question— "How shall this be, for I know not man?"—appeals for the sending of the Spirit "from on high" and for the overshadowing of the power of the Most High which will make possible the coming of "the Son of God."

Not for a second does Mary lift herself up. She stays exactly in her place as creature, perfectly small and humble. She is the Lowest One who is to give birth to the Most High. She is the "servant of the Lord," totally at the service of His Word. She is aware that God is about to pronounce, in His Incarnate Son, His ultimate creative word concerning man, the world and the Father. With an unerring instinct that comes from the Spirit, she senses, foresees even, that this Word will be the great, astounding, disconcerting and wonderful Word of the Cross and Resurrection, with its flowing tide of blood and flooding streams of love. To this Love, to this burning *Agapé* of the Holy Trinity, she utters the total "Yes" for which she has been prepared.

It is in this way, as a creature who freely says "Yes," a servant who takes her share in the service of her Son, that she inaugurates her maternal reign and takes the path that leads towards her Son's divine sovereignty.

The young girl who encountered the angel assumes, at the moment of the Annunciation, all her noble dignity. Having remained until then in the shadow of the pure divine light, she begins to appear in the history of men as it is guided by God's plan. At one and the same time, she is revealed in this plan, both in her secret, intimate conse-cration as the Immaculate one, and in her unique mission as Mother of God.

The Pope and Mary Immaculate

The second panel—we can position it on the other side, the counterpart and echo of the first—shows us quite a different scene: an immense crowd gathered at the Vati-can, a ray of light falling on a pope who is proclaiming a dogma of faith.

Eighteen centuries have passed, and another messenger utters the young girl's name. Pius IX has been Pope since 1846. He has had to face the Roman revolution which obliged him to flee to Gaète barely two years after his election. It was in this city, then situated in the territories belonging to the Kingdom of Naples, that he wrote his encyclical letter *Ubi primum*, in which he asked for the opinion of the Catholic episcopacy on whether or not to define the dogma of Our Lady's Immaculate Conception. This extensive consultation followed steps taken from the very beginning of his pontificate, in particular the nomination of a commission of theologians. Since the time of his predecessor, Gregory XVI, numerous national episcopates had sent requests to Rome expressing the wish for Our Lady's great privilege to be proclaimed. It was clear that the encyclical struck a chord: 546 positive replies were received out of 603. The long and delicate task of drawing up a Bull of definition was then undertaken. A first, and then a second, draft were rejected. A third draft was studied at length: it provided the core for the definitive text, which, after five revisions, was finally submitted to a commission of twenty one cardinals who decided upon the final text itself in November 1854. It was this document that was submitted for the approval of the Consistory which gathered on 1 December. One last meeting of the Pope with seven cardinals on 4 December made it possible for the finishing touches to be added.

The promulgation of the dogma took place on 8 December 1854 at a vast ceremony in Saint Peter's Basilica. After a long, solemn procession, the Holy Father began the High Mass. Immediately after the incensing of the altar and the singing of the *Veni Creator*, the Pope pronounced the decree of the dogmatic definition. A witness recounted:

When the Pope reached the solemn words: "For the greater glory of the Mother of God, by the authority of the holy Apostles Peter and Paul and by our own," pierced by the immensity of what he was doing . . . the Sovereign Pontiff was aware of his voice faltering and his eyes filling with tears. But making an effort to control himself and overcome his emotion, he continued in a firm voice, then, after giving way a second time to being overwhelmed, he continued reading the decree amidst a feeling of universal joy. There was one thing to which all the witnesses testify. . . . "During the proclamation of the dogma it was raining heavily; now, at the very moment when the Pontiff pronounced the words of the definition, the clouds parted and a ray of light shone upon the Pontiff."

As for the Pope himself, he confided to a religious sister who asked him about it:

Perhaps, my child, you think that the pope was rapt in ecstasy, and that Mary appeared to him at that moment? . . . Ah, no, I had no ecstasy or vision or anything like that, but what I experienced, what I learned when I defined that dogma, was such as no human tongue could ever express.

When I began to publish the dogmatic decree, I felt quite incapable of making my voice heard by the immense crowd thronging the Vatican Basilica, but when I reached the actual formula of the definition, God gave his Vicar's voice such strength and such supernatural vigour that the entire Basilica resounded with it. And this divine succour made such a profound impression on me that I was obliged to be silent for a moment and give free rein to my tears.

Moreover, while God proclaimed the dogma by the mouth of his Vicar, God Himself gave my spirit such a clear and extensive understanding of the Most Holy Virgin's incomparable purity, that, plunged in the depths of this understanding, which no language can describe, my soul remained flooded with unutterable delight, such delight as does not belong to this world and which one can only experience in Heaven. No earthly wealth or joy can give anyone the least idea of this delight, and I am not afraid to affirm that the Vicar of Christ needed a special grace in order not to die of delight given the impression this experience made upon him, this knowledge and awareness of the incomparable beauty of Mary Immaculate. (cf. Pierre Fernessole, Pie IX, tome 1, 264–67)

This brief sketch of the historical context for the ceremony of 8 December 1854 brings us directly to a meditation on the actual text of the dogmatic definition:

> We declare, enunciate and define that the doctrine which teaches that the Blessed Virgin Mary, from the very first moment of her Conception, was, by a special grace and privilege of Almighty God, in view of the foreseen merits of Jesus Christ, the Savior of the human race, preserved and exempt from all stain of original sin, is a doctrine revealed by God, and which must therefore be firmly and steadfastly believed by all the faithful.

Every word in such a definition has been carefully weighed.

The Immaculate Conception is defined as "a doctrine revealed by God." The text does not specify in what way, whether explicitly or implicitly, this revelation is found in Scripture and tradition. We know that the theologians relied chiefly on the Church's practice, in this case the very ancient celebration of the feast of Our Lady's Conception.

Mary was preserved from sin "from the first instance of her Conception." The preparatory texts had spoken of the preservation of Mary's soul from the moment of its creation and its infusion into her body. In the end, they avoided this vocabulary, too inclined, perhaps, towards certain philosophic positions. It was decided to speak of the Virgin Mary. It was she herself who was the object of this privilege, not just her soul, and this from the very first moment of her existence.

It was from this first moment that she was "preserved and exempt from all stain of original sin." The Council of Trent, dealing with original sin (17 June 1546), had already expressly declared that it had no intention of including the case of the Virgin Mary in the universality of original sin. It referred back to previous texts, especially the Constitution *Grave nimis* of Sixtus IV (4 September 1483), which had prohibited teaching that the Virgin Mary had been conceived with original sin. Pius IX stated quite specifically that Mary had not only been exempt from original sin—which could just have been the simple assertion of an absence—but that she was absolutely preserved from it—which constitutes a certain kind of explanation. "Mary," Duns Scotus already used to say, "would have contracted original sin by reason of her ordinary human origin, had this not been prevented by the grace of our divine Mediator." We can thus understand that Mary was filled with grace and with supernatural life.

This preservation and exemption are the effect of a "singular grace and privilege of almighty God." The intention here is not so much to indicate a deviation from the universal law of original sin as to point towards a special favor granted to Mary. Although it is not explicitly stated, we are allowed to think that this privilege is unique, in spite of recurrent attempts to attribute a similar privilege to Saint Joseph.

The source of this privilege is expressed thus: "by the foreseen merits of Jesus Christ, the Savior of the human race." Mary's purity finds its source in the purity of her Son. While for him it is innate, for Mary it is acquired by the merits of Christ. We may therefore speak in this sense of Mary's redemption, as Pius XII would say in his encyclical *Fulgens Corona* (1953): "Christ the Lord in a certain most perfect manner really redeemed His mother, since it was by virtue of His merits that she was preserved by God immune from all stain of original sin."

While he was proclaiming Mary preserved from all stain of sin, Pope Pius IX received the grace of a very special understanding of Mary's purity. Faith tells us that there is no stain in Mary. Grace enables us to understand: she is all pure, full of light, completely penetrated with the radiance of the divinity. She is all this in relation to, and in total dependence upon, her Son, through him and because of him. She is the most perfect mirror of the supreme holiness of her Son, the Word Incarnate, God made flesh.

God and the Woman

We come now to the central panel, where Mary Immaculate stands in all her majesty, virtually as she appears on the miraculous medal: ruling over the world, treading the serpent under foot, she sheds rays of heavenly graces upon the earth.

The face which the Angel gazed upon and which the Pope contemplated echoes a still more penetrating vision: that of God Himself, the gaze the Father turns towards

Mary. This gaze reaches back in time; in a certain sense it always was. In any event, it preceded and laid the foundation for what the Angel and the Pope, and all those after them who have seen and believed, have contemplated.

One of the very first texts in the Bible bears witness to this vision. In fact, tradition recognised a prophecy of the Immaculate Conception in the celebrated 3rd chapter of Genesis, verse 15.

After the fall, God comes as usual to walk in the garden in the evening. He no longer finds Adam, who is hiding himself. He searches for him: "Where are you?" The man admits his fear: he has hidden himself because he knows that he is naked. And God makes a little inquiry. "It was the woman," says the man. "It was the serpent," says the woman. Then judgement is pronounced. The first judgement falls upon the serpent: "cursed are you above all beasts, and above all wild animals; upon your belly you shall go, and dust you shall eat all the days of your life. I will put enmity between you and the woman, and between your seed and her seed; he shall bruise your head, and you shall bruise his heel."

Exegetical tradition has called this text the "Protogospel," that is, the first Gospel. In fact, the tradition sees, in these lines, the foretelling of a combat which would finally see the victory of the man's descendants over those of the serpent.

The Greek translation bears witness to this very ancient interpretation. It employs a masculine pronoun for the one who "will bruise your head," while the term it refers to—lineage—is neuter in Greek. Thus, it is not only the victory of his lineage in general that is foretold, but rather of one masculine member of this lineage. There is every reason to believe that we have here a re-reading of the text in the light of messianic hope. The one who is mysteriously designated would indeed be the Messiah, "Son of Adam, Son of God," as Saint Luke would put it. (Lk. 3:38)

The Latin version of Saint Jerome's Vulgate goes even further by employing a feminine pronoun: "I will put enmity between you and the woman, and between your seed and her seed; she shall bruise your head, and you shall bruise her heel."

Through the victory of the descendant of the woman's lineage, Jerome's translation contemplates the victory of the woman herself. This development could seem bold, something tacked on by subsequent Marian belief, but we should rather consider it as a homogeneous evolution and a happy and enlightened explanation. The opposition between the woman and the serpent concerns not so much the daughters of Eve considered one by one—men too being enemies of the serpent and vice versa—as another woman, the new Eve, who in messianic times confronts the serpent's blasphemous challenge. Intimately associated with the combat and victory of her Son, Mary, the Mother of God, is *the* Woman *par excellence*, summing up in herself all women since Eve. She incarnates the eternal feminine as she exists eternally in God's plan of love. Thus, Mary surpasses Eve as the perfect type of feminine humanity, just as Jesus, the new Adam, is the perfect man. Saint Jerome's tradition shows us how the Church loved to contemplate Mary's eternal predestination as "Woman," indissolubly linked to the predestination of Christ himself.

The text of Genesis reveals to us the eternal vision, design and will of God. God looks upon Adam and Eve in their fallen state; He sees the immense suffering that will be the inevitable consequence of their sin. Yet we may say that He sees this man and woman in the light of the perfect Man, Jesus, and the Woman *par excellence*, Mary. In other words, the Father sees further than the fall. He sees the victory which will not only restore the equilibrium which man's sin had destabilized, but will shed light on His reason for allowing the fall at all. God let the fall take place without allowing it to make his excellent plan fail, because He knew He would be able to draw victory and the highest glory out of fallen humanity's very lineage, and in this He could make His divinity better known and praised.

Thus the divine promise of the woman's ultimate victory over the serpent rests on the divine contemplation of Mary. Standing beside the Son of God made flesh, foreign to sin by nature, God has always seen and foreseen Mary, the all-pure one, foreign to sin by grace. If Our Lady of Sorrows suffers during her Son's Passion at one level of her being—symbolised by the heel in the prophecy of

Genesis—she crushes the serpent underfoot by her perfect purity which renders her impervious to the devil's temptations.

Immaculate and, as such, redeemed by the merits of her Son, she is the Mother of God who will exercise her maternity towards all humanity, regenerated in the paschal sacrifice of the Only Son. Thus, the All-Pure One's vocation is one of collaboration with the redemption. Mary simultaneously has a place beside her Son and is in constant dependence upon Him, a sharer in the suffering of men's sins. Not that she herself is a sinner; her very preservation from sin renders her totally dependent upon the Father and docile to his redemptive will. She is "handmaid of the Lord" by her very vocation, not simply in order to be present at the beginning of the Savior's humanity, but truly to be a Mother for the entire Church and for all humanity, which is called to be, through her, regenerated in the Passover of the Son of God.

From the very beginning—or better, from all eternity—the Father looked at Mary. The words of the Book of Proverbs, which the liturgy applies to her so readily, suit her perfectly: "Ages ago I was set up, at the first, before the beginning of the earth. When there were no depths I was brought forth." (8:23–24) Or, again, those words of Sirach: "From eternity, in the beginning, he created me, and for eternity I shall not cease to exist." (24:9) In these texts, it is not a question of making Mary an eternal creature in herself, a sort of goddess, but of perceiving the place Mary has always had in the supremely wise divine plan.

Mary, "Seat of Wisdom" according to the Litany of Loretto, is the created mirror of eternal Wisdom, the Word of God who became her Son at the Annunciation. Absolutely unacquainted with sin, she is entirely enveloped in God's light and love from the first moment of her creation. The believer's gaze, admiring her luminous beauty, may let itself be guided in perfect safety by the Angel's words, by the Pope's definition and by the judgement pronounced by God the Father.

II

The Mother of
Mary Immaculate

From the Gospels to the Apocrypha

WE CANNOT SEPARATE OUR LADY'S IMMACULATE Conception from the one who was her mother, and whom tradition has called Saint Anne. The Gospel tells us nothing about Mary's birth. It leaves many questions unanswered: what tribe she belonged to—was she of the tribe of David like her husband Joseph, or of the tribe of Levi like her cousin Elizabeth?—but also her parents, her education, how she met Joseph to whom she would be engaged. In its purity and sobriety, the Gospel says just enough to enable the believers' contemplation, stirred up by the Holy Spirit in the Church, to see the mystery appear in the harmony of the faith. Saint Luke's phrase "full of grace" is enough for the believing gaze to encounter the mystery of the Immaculate Conception.

The Church knows how to render the truth she sees in the brevity of the Gospel text accessible to all by presenting it in the form of more extensive accounts. One of the forms early Christian contemplation took was the compilation of texts to complement the Gospel; this was how many of the apocryphal gospels came into existence. They are not the word of God and do not belong to the Canon of Scripture, but they do have a place in Tradition in the broad sense, as a meditation, more or less authorized according to circumstances, a collection of images which express certain aspects of the mysteries of the faith. The historical or theological truth of these texts is not guaranteed. They must be submitted to prudent examination. But they bear witness to the way believers strive, in prayer and in listening to the resonances of the Word of God, to understand the mystery.

Nascent Christianity soon had detractors. Thinkers, sometimes powerful ones like the pagan philosopher Celsus, against whom Origen had to defend the Church's faith, denied any truth in the Gospel narratives. In his *True Discourses* published about 178, Celsus maintained that Jesus was the child of an adulterous relationship between his mother—a woman of very low birth, a peasant girl, a poor thread spinner—and a Roman soldier named Panther. After being repudiated by her husband, a carpenter by trade, Mary would have wandered shamefully about and given birth to her son in secret. Coming from just any little hamlet in Judea, Jesus himself would have invented the story of his birth from a virgin. The reader can see how attempts to reduce the life of Jesus to a simple human story, to ridicule it, are as old as the Church. One way for Christians to reply to these attacks was to spread more complete versions of the story of Jesus's origins and to place them under the authority of one or other of the Apostles.

Thus the Apocryphal Gospels were at once a reply to certain objections and the fruit of the Church's contemplation of the mysteries of Christ. Among them we encounter a text with a remarkable history. Since the 16th century, it has circulated under the title of "Proto-evangelium of James," but in Christian antiquity it was usually known by the title "The Nativity of Mary." The word *Proto-evangelium* does not signify here, as it does for the text of Genesis 3:15, the idea of the first announcement of salvation. Rather, it signifies an account of events that took place immediately before the events recounted in the Canonical Gospels. Already known by authors such as Clement of Alexandria (who lived in the 2nd century) and Origen (†254), this text played a not inconsiderable role in the development of Mariology and supplied the foundations for related iconography. It was used in the liturgy—more frequently in the East, where church leaders were more circumspect with regard to canonicity than in the West—and traces of its influence can still be found therein. It lies behind such feasts as the Presentation of Our Lady and, most notably, the ancient feast of Saint Anne's Conceiving, which was be the Church's remote preparation for the feast of the Immaculate Conception.

The Story in the Protogospel

Let us call to mind the main lines of the story. Joachim is a very rich man of Jerusalem who makes magnificent gifts to the temple. One day, when he comes to present his offering, he hears the following reproach: "You are not allowed to be the first to bring your offerings, because you have not fathered any offspring in Israel." Having consulted the ancient traditions of his people, he realises that having children is a distinctive characteristic of just men. Deeply grieved, he withdraws into the desert for a complete fast of forty days.

During this time, Anne can only lament: she has not had a child and thinks that her husband has disappeared. She suffers the mockery of her servant girl, but soon turns towards God. Just as Joachim, in his prayer, reminds us of Abraham, Anne calls to mind before God her "Mother, Sarah." Then, in her grief, she gives utterance to a beautiful speech. It is at this moment that she receives a visit from an angel:

> And behold, an angel of the Lord stood before her, saying: "Anne, Anne, the Lord God has heard your prayer. You will conceive and bear a child, and people will speak about your offspring throughout the whole world." And Anne said: "As surely as the Lord God lives, if I bear a child, whether it is a boy or a girl, I will bring it as an offering to the Lord my God, and it will be at his service all the days of its life."

For his part, Joachim had also been visited by an angel:

> "Joachim, Joachim, the Lord God has heard your prayer. Depart from here. Behold your wife Anne has conceived in her womb." On hearing this news, Joachim returned in haste to the city, bearing offerings for the temple. And behold, Joachim arrived with his flocks. Anne was waiting at the city gates and saw Joachim coming with his flocks. At once she ran and embraced him, saying: "Now I know that the Lord God has blessed me enormously. Behold, the widow is no longer a widow, and I the barren one have conceived in my womb." And Joachim spent that first day at home. (4:4)

About six months pass, and in the seventh month Anne bears her child. "She said to the midwife: 'What have I borne?' And the midwife answered, 'A daughter.' And Anne said 'My soul is lifted up this day.' And she laid her down. And, when the days were accomplished, Anne was cleansed from her impurity, suckled her child and called her name Mary." (5:2)

The general meaning of such a story is clear: Mary's birth involves a special divine intervention. To express this, the writer draws on the extant treasury of biblical narratives. We often meet miraculous births in the Bible; they are the prelude to the exceptional missions of the children thus conceived. Since the days of Abraham and Sarah, the birth of an heir to God's friends has been closely connected with a special divine intervention.

Where childbearing is humanly impossible—often in the case of a barren, elderly couple—God comes to bestow a special blessing.

Fertility is the blessing most intimately connected with the original creative word: "Increase and multiply." To have no children can seem a punishment, a curse. Yet the Bible frequently depicts good people, men and women whose devotion to and fear of God is emphasized, who struggle with infertility. These stories consider barrenness from a new angle: it is no longer a divine punishment, but a test. It leads the couple in question either to welcome humbly, in courageous faith, the gift of a descendant that God freely gives them—as seen in the case of such couples as Abraham and Sarah, or Zachariah and Elizabeth— or to immerse themselves in confident prayer for a miracle, as does Hannah, the mother of little Samuel. In the latter case, those who ask often promise to consecrate their miraculous fruit to the Lord. It is as though the parents must be ready to make more of an offering of the child given to them miraculously by placing the child completely at God's disposal. Their barrenness paves the way to their asking God for the child in complete dependence upon Him, offering the child back to Him at once. Barrenness, lived in faith and in abandonment to God's love, thus participates in the miraculous fecundity of the Cross, according to the Biblical—and, more particularly the Christian—law that it is in apparent human failure that God accomplishes the victory of His mercy.

The text's insistence on Joachim and Anne's righteousness is very much in keeping with all this. Even righteousness, and an exemplary righteousness at that, does not automatically give one a right to fruitfulness, which is always God's merciful blessing. It does not follow that righteousness is of no value or has no merit in God's eyes, still less that the righteous are always so proud that God must first humble them before He can hear their prayers. We must, rather, understand that righteousness itself is an effect of God's merciful kindness appearing in man.

Thus, all is mercy, and the profound meaning of the miraculous births, long awaited by a barren couple, which punctuate the biblical narrative of both Testaments goes to show that this mercy is even more at work where sanctity—whether that of the parents, or of the child, or of both at the same time—is particularly outstanding. A saint is a masterpiece, a gift of mercy. Saints can appear suddenly in an ordinary family. Often they are preceded by a whole line of ancestors who bear them and prepare for them, just as a good tree can one day bear excellent fruit. This preparation itself is mercy's gift.

The Protogospel's account of Mary's miraculous conception can thus be understood as an expression of the following conviction: that she who was the Mother of God by a virginal conception and birth was herself from the very beginning, from the root, so to speak, of her being, the object of divine mercy's special attention. Her birth was already a sign destined to direct hearts towards the merciful action of God, who was preparing for the Savior's coming.

Mary is the fruit of her parents' prayers and of divine mercy. A special indication of this truth appears in her premature birth, understood as a proof of God's action. Nevertheless, one expression in the text creates a problem. Anne cries out: "Behold, the widow is no longer a widow, and I the barren one have conceived in my womb." Are we to understand that she conceived without the natural intervention of her spouse, and thus in a virginal way? This is, perhaps, what the writer wanted us to imagine. However, the traditional interpretation is unanimous in giving the text a prophetic meaning, by which Anne celebrates in the present something that is to happen in the future. This tradition has always denied that Mary's own birth was virginal; it is understood that such a conception could only be Jesus's privilege.

You may have noticed that our apocryphal text does not explicitly mention the doctrine of the Immaculate Conception, an omission which could disappoint us. Instead, we should be glad that the author has shrouded Mary's conception in mystery. By this account (and those which continue it: the Infancy Gospel of Pseudo-Matthew and the Book of the Nativity of Mary), we find preserved in Christian faith and imagination the necessary room for the dogma of faith. The feast of Anne's Conceiving would become that of the Immaculate Conception, and this evolution bears witness to a deepening of Christian contemplation. But from the

Protogospel of James, the *sensus fidelium* testifies that one cannot say of Mary that she had either an ordinary birth or an ordinary conception. Its biblical terms and images—the barren, yet saintly couple, the angelic messages, the premature birth—all provide a strong affirmation of Mary's special holiness from her very origin.

Anne and Mary: The Conception

Mary's holiness, signified by the ancient feast of Anne's conceiving—a feast observed principally in the East, but testified to in the West—would, little by little, be made more explicit by theologians, who, not without sometimes very heated discussions, would formulate the doctrine of the Immaculate Conception in an ever more precise and reasoned way.

Leaving this development of doctrine on one side, let us stay close to Saint Anne. The heart of the believer may well strive to fathom the exceptional relationship that existed between Anne and Mary. Whatever the exact historical circumstances were, and they will always remain unknown to us, it seems hardly likely that the Immaculate Virgin's mother was totally ignorant of her child's special privilege. Furthermore, their relationship was certainly unique, belonging, on the one hand, to them alone—entirely enveloped in the silence that surrounds them, a silence heavy with mystery—and, on the other hand, to the treasury of the Church's life, which compels us to contemplate it with respect and love.

Two women, one facing the other: a mother and her daughter. Are they not, in a special way, within one another? For the mother bears the daughter and the daughter resembles her mother. There exists between them a profound continuity of life, a physical continuity, a continuity of the creative act. From the very beginning, God unites them as He unites every mother and daughter.

Consider Anne. Tradition sees her as elderly and barren. This barren old woman is the symbol of a world. She represents a humanity quite incapable of giving life. For, we might ask, to give a life inexorably doomed to suffering and death—a life necessarily marked by sin—is that really giving life in the most profound sense? Should not the woman's child, if it is to live, rather proceed from grace to grace towards a fullness that will enable it to enter naturally, as it were, into the divine life? Every woman—and, in her, our world marked by sin—may be called barren of true life, of authentic childbearing. Therefore every child must be "reborn," "born from above," as Jesus will explain to Nicodemus. (Jn. 3:3)

Consider Mary. This woman is youth itself. In her, beginning with her, the ancient world is radically transformed from within in order that the new creation may appear, the new man, a creation and a man in perfect harmony with God's own life.

Is the continuity between Anne and Mary, the relationship between them, merely biological? No. The Holy Spirit unites them. He who "is the Lord, the giver of life" visited Saint Anne's heart and body. Long before that, he visited, animated, guided her desire. A woman who longs for a child longs to give life. She has a legitimate desire to give the most beautiful, the most noble, the richest life. She longs to give the fullness of life. This desire is pregnant with immense hope: in it, the woman looks towards God, asking Him to give life, with her and in her. The life of the child that is to be born is situated on the horizons of her desire, it is true, but, in the hope of divine salvation, her desire grows: may this child be a source of life for the world! For Saint Anne the Jewess, as for every woman of her race, her hope extends to the longing to be the mother of the Messiah. And this is perfectly normal, for every woman feels obscurely that she has a mission to give life to the world, to carry the new world in her heart and in her body.

As always in Christianity, the physical and the spiritual coincide. Woman lives out, in the unity of her body and heart, of her flesh and spirit, her great mission at the service of life. It is not the child that makes the mother, but the maternal heart that puts itself at the service of a new life—whether this motherhood is lived out physically, as is more usual, or, according to a possibility that is specifically Christian, on the spiritual plane, opening up whole vistas of fulfilment in the deepest being of a virgin or a single woman, as it does for a married woman unable to have children or to one who has ceased to have children.

Saint Anne is thus totally given over to the Holy Spirit,

the sole Author of fecundity. Within her conjugal relationship with Saint Joachim, she commits all her faith, hope and love to a fully spiritual conception, a completely free motherhood ready to be filled with and moved by the breath of the Spirit. And one can certainly affirm that there was, in the heart of both Saint Anne and Saint Joachim, a free and joyful consent to the greater, more profound action of the Holy Spirit in the conception of their child Mary. Anne's trial, which was to bear in her flesh the barrenness of our world, had prepared her to put herself humbly at the Spirit's disposal, ready for a fruitfulness that she could only receive from him and which would more than fulfil her deepest longings as a woman and a mother. And it is this heart, entirely open to the infinite possibilities of the grace of the Holy Spirit, which committed itself to collaborate fully with the amazing work of divine mercy.

Saint Anne, a barren woman called by pure grace to conceive, stands before us as an expert in mercy. She has received from the faith of her ancestors infinite confidence in the resources of divine mercy. In this sense, her name suits her perfectly, to the point where one might well ask: could the mother of Mary Immaculate be called anything but Anne, a name which signifies precisely divine grace, the completely free and merciful favour of the Almighty?

Anne's view of Mary and Mary's of Anne thus contain, within the physical bond which unites mother and daughter, a privileged contemplation of divine mercy. In one and the same Holy Spirit, they admire in each other the work of the Father, each humbling herself before the other, and both before God "rich in mercy." (Eph. 2:4) The ancient, graced world, represented by Anne, greets in Mary the new world of pure grace. The Immaculate Heart of Mary looks at and loves her holy mother Anne, who is a living and joyful celebration of divine mercy.

Furthermore, the looks that they exchange open out and ceaselessly reach towards the future, for these two women are two links in a chain that leads towards Christ. In their whole being, body and soul, they are orientated towards him. Their pure hearts are filled with the memory of divine mercy, and are therefore upheld by the highest hope. They perceive that they bear the first fruits of a world renewed by mercy. On their path of faith, along which they advance daily through the shadows of this life, they are aware of just how close God's decisive work is. They are totally at His disposal for the accomplishment of this work.

Anne and Mary: The Presentation

This availability is symbolically expressed by the traditional account of Our Lady's Presentation in the Temple. Already, according to the Protogospel, Anne had made her room a sanctuary, a place most pure. But when Mary was three years old, she was led by her parents to the Temple in Jerusalem:

The priest received her, and having embraced her, blessed her and said: "The Lord God has exalted your name through all generations. In you, in the last days, the Lord will manifest his redemption to the children of Israel." And he placed her of the third step of the altar. And the Lord made his grace come down upon her. And her feet began to dance, and all the house of Israel loved her. And her parents returned, full of wonder, praising and glorifying God, the Master, because she did not turn back to look at them. Now, Mary, like a dove, remained in the Temple of the Lord and received food from the hand of an angel. (7:7–10, 8:1–2)

Mary remains in the place of meeting between God and men. She is placed on one of the steps of the altar of sacrifice. Like little Samuel long ago, she waits for God's hour. She is at his disposal, ready to render Him the service he will ask of her, a service that will prove sacrificial. She will live it out according to her femininity, to the rhythm of the successive stages of her existence. It is thus that she will first become Joseph's spouse. Then, according to the Protogospel, she will be appointed to weave the purple and scarlet veil for the Temple—a detail from which originates the use of the colour red for Mary's clothing in the Eastern iconographic tradition. From the moment of the Annunciation, it is precisely as woman and mother that she will serve the redemptive plan: she will be the woman who gives birth to the new world at the foot of her Son's cross, as also in the upper room of Pentecost.

In the apocryphal accounts, Anne and Joachim disappear from the scene once Mary has been presented in the temple. There is no description in these traditions of any touching family reunions bringing together the various generations. Anne never plays the role of Jesus's grandmother. She remains "Mary's mother," and it is as Mary's mother that she presents herself to Yvon Nicolazic in 1725 at Auray in Brittany. This discreet self-effacement is part and parcel of her motherhood, which is perfectly free and entirely self-giving. The child of grace is only given to her in order that she, in her turn might give her completely to the Lord, as in the beautiful prayer of Hannah, the mother of Samuel: "It was for this child that I prayed and the Lord has granted me the request I made of him. I in my turn give him to the Lord; as long as he lives, he is given to the Lord." (1 Sam. 1:27–28)

The feminine heart's capacity for giving, magnificently realised by the Virgin Mary at the foot of the cross, is realised by Saint Anne in Our Lady's Presentation. The mother has given life, and she offers her child to God. Mary Immaculate cannot be separated from the humble maternal service of Saint Anne, who gave her very self to the work of grace and offered to God the fruit of her womb. From Anne to Mary and to Jesus, we thus contemplate a kind of genealogy of grace, which, by ascending degrees, constantly embraces the form of redemptive ser-

vice in an ever more demanding way. It would perhaps
have been moving to contemplate Saint Anne as a good-
natured granny. We can thank the Church's spiritual tradition for presenting her to us as a woman who enters, with
all the richness of her maternal heart, into the mystery of
redemptive sacrifice out of which the new world is to be
born.

III

The Mercy Stairway

T HE IMMACULATE CONCEPTION IS A MYSTERY OF mercy. According to the text of the Bull defining the dogma, the Blessed Virgin Mary "was pre-served free from all stain of original sin from the very first moment of her Conception, by a singular grace and privilege of Almighty God, in view of the merits of Jesus Christ, the Savior of the human race." Like all the elect, Mary was saved by Christ, yet she was saved in a super-eminent way. In her, mercy anticipated the work of salva-tion, not only by preserving her from faults during the course of her life, but even by separating her, at her beginning, from all involvement in the world of sin. By sheer mercy, Mary was saved from sin and from the world of sin from the first instant of her conception.

In order to more fully understand this great and beauti-ful truth, each one of us can undertake the ascent of what one might call "The Mercy Stairway." It consists of three steps. On the first, we meet Mary Magdalen, the forgiven sinner who becomes the beloved, the preferred one. Then, little Thérèse brings us to the second step: that of innocence, whose profound relationship with divine mercy she fathoms, precisely by situating herself alongside the one she calls "*la Madeleine*." Then, at the top of the stairs the Immaculate Virgin can appear in full light. On this final step, she enables us to understand how the unique privilege of her Immaculate Conception places her at the very heart of the Father's merciful dispensation. The Sinner and the Innocent One thus lead us to the Immaculate one who is totally attentive to us "poor sinners."

The Sinner

With the whole spiritual tradition from Saint Gregory the Great onwards, we consider as one and the same the loving forgiven sinner of Luke 7:36–50, Mary of Bethany who anointed the feet of Jesus on the eve of his passion (Jn. 11:2 and 12:1–18), and Mary Magdalen, who had been delivered from seven demons (Lk. 8:2), who followed Jesus and ministered to him from Galilee as far as Calvary (Mt. 27:55–56; Mk. 16:40–41; Lk. 23:49; Jn. 19:25), who came to the tomb early in the morning (Mt. 28:1–10), to whom the Lord appeared first of all (Jn. 20:1–10) charging her to be the first messenger of his resurrection to the apostles (Jn. 20: 11–18), entitling her to be called the Apostle of the Apostles.

Since the last liturgical reforms, two different dates honour Mary of Bethany, whose feast is, on the one hand, celebrated with that of Martha and Lazarus on 29 July, and, on the other hand, on 22 July with Mary Magdalene. So it is not on the exegesis itself—which is divided on the question anyway—nor on the liturgy that we shall rely, but on the spiritual tradition, which, not without exegetical grounds, has loved to consider as one and the same this great sinner turned disciple, using her resources to help Jesus, who honours her with a very special friendship. This loving and faithful woman had the double privilege of finding herself with Mary at the foot of the Cross of Jesus and of being the first to whom he revealed himself after his Resurrection.

Thus, Mary Magdalen appears at the outset as the sinner *par excellence*. Jesus drove seven devils out of her, which is a way of saying that she was profoundly marked by evil, totally corrupt. In circumstances of which we are ignorant, Jesus delivered her from her deep-seated involvement with evil and from the Evil One's authority over her life and person. This fact was so well known to the first generation of Christians that the Evangelists did not consider it necessary to consign the matter to writing. It was, after all, only the point of departure.

In contrast to so many other people in the Gospel cured by Jesus, of whose subsequent lives we know nothing, the Evangelists have discreetly transmitted to us the Magdalen story, which is, in fact, a magnificent love story. This is not to say that there was between Jesus and the Magdalen a sensual or sentimental love affair such as contemporary authors would have us imagine—taking up nothing other than errors already enunciated in antiquity by the gnostic apocryphal work entitled the Gospel of Philip. But there did exist between Magdalen and the Savior a spiritual encounter of love that led Mary Magdalen to the highest mystical intimacy with the Lord.

Such is indeed the profound meaning of the traditional presentation of only one Mary Magdalen. If the greatest sinner, who represented in some way the sinner *par excellence,* was delivered by Jesus and led by him to the summit of mystical union, we may be sure that every sinner, however far removed he may be from God, may, by the Lord's merciful grace, not only be re-established in divine friendship, but be gratuitously invited to the most intimate union with his God.

Mary Magdalen's great, outstanding accomplishment is the fervor of her love. She is the one who loves; if she has known the lowest depths of carnal love, the wretchedness of a love hopelessly astray in its object, this was only so that she could be graciously invited to true love, and in order that she might occupy a lofty place there. There is but one step from the darkness of sin to the glory of spiritual marriage. Magdalen, the great lover, took that step, swept along by divine mercy.

This is what the unforgettable scene recounted by Saint Luke symbolises. A sinner from the city comes to find Jesus while he is at table in the house of Simon the Pharisee: "She brought an alabaster flask of ointment, and standing behind him at his feet, weeping, she began to wet his feet with her tears, and wiped them with the hair of her head, and kissed his feet, and anointed them with the ointment." (Lk. 7:37–38) The Pharisee then reflects that, if Jesus were a prophet, he would know what sort of woman was touching him. Jesus tells him the story of the two debtors, making him understand that one who has been forgiven more loves more. In this parable, love is considered as a consequence of forgiveness.

Then, Jesus makes a statement concerning the woman: "You have not... she has..." with its conclusion: "Therefore I tell you, her sins, which are many, are forgiven, for she loved much." This woman who was sorry for her many sins, covered her sorrow with penitent love. She went to Jesus as to one who made present the God she had offended by her sins and the God to whom she wanted to show her love. In this scene, love precedes forgiveness.

Magdalen is found at the meeting place of two loves, both bound in different ways to the forgiveness of sins. Repentant love—which corresponds to what theology has called perfect contrition—is the love which precedes forgiveness. Under the action of grace, the heart turns towards God with a sorrowful love that suffers from having grieved the loved one. This is the love which Jesus praises and which obtains for Mary Magdalen the forgiveness of her sins.

Yet the forgiveness of sins frees and strengthens love, which then becomes a love marked by special gratitude towards divine mercy.

These two loves explain Mary Magdalen's gesture: it is with a heart bruised by love that she approaches Jesus and carries out on his body the gestures of ardent love, filled with a repentant and humble spirit. From this, she passes imperceptibly, as her trust and her hope of pardon increase, to the expression of a grateful love which takes the form of a sumptuous rite in honour of the beloved. Thus we must understand the proceedings: first the tears, then the perfume.

This daring gesture of love, extremely humble and completely unheard of—it is the head that one anoints and not the feet, and who would use their hair for drying?—made a vivid impression on Jesus's first disciples. It remained associated with this woman's personality. That is why it has traditionally been linked to another anointing—the one Jesus received on the eve of his Passion. Matthew and Mark speak of a woman who broke an alabaster vase and poured precious ointment on Jesus's head. John presents things otherwise: "Mary took a pound of costly ointment of pure nard, and anointed the feet of Jesus and wiped them with her hair." (Jn. 12:3) This time, there are no tears, but a sumptuous gesture, the pure overflowing of loving tenderness. Nevertheless, this love once again takes the unusual form of an anointing of Jesus's feet, accompanied by wiping with her hair.

The converted penitent's love, that of one who has become very dear to the Lord, is lifted into a new dimension by Christ's solemn declaration. It remains in continuity with the first anointing which it reminds us of. But Jesus's words set it against the ultimate horizon of the burial of his own body. His words establish a link between his death, the forgiveness of sins, and Mary Magdalen's love for the Savior.

Light is only shed on this mysterious scene by the darkness of the Cross. There, the evangelists are unanimous in underlining the fidelity of certain women. Matthew, Mark and John name Mary Magdalen, while John is the only one to also mention Mary the Mother of Jesus. All these women represent the fidelity of love, in its various forms: the maternal love of Mary, the love of sisters and disciples represented by the other Marys, and the love of mystical marriage as represented by Mary Magdalen. Love does not allow itself to be reduced to dumb contemplation of the terrible sufferings of the Passion; hearts that love find themselves associated in a privileged way with the love of the Savior. Thus the penitent is invited to share in the Cross, to participate in the sacrifice of the Lamb who takes away the sins of the world. She is led to the very source of mercy: the pierced Heart of Christ, overflowing with love.

On the morning of Easter Day, we find Mary Magdalen at Christ's tomb. She experiences the surprise of the empty tomb, the awesome appearance of the angels, the hurried journey of Peter and John, the grief of her beloved Lord's absence. Distraught, she searches for him, and, as soon as the "gardener" pronounces her name, she throws herself at his feet, ever faithful to a gesture that marks her out in a special way in her relationship with the

Lord. But it is no longer the time to take hold of Jesus's body. While Mary Magdalen is sent to the Church to proclaim to it the Resurrection, she is also directed towards the Father as towards the ultimate source of mercy; it is to Him that Jesus is ascending.

Spiritual authors—such as Bérulle in his *Elévation sur Sainte Madeleine*, or more recently, Lacordaire in his *Sainte Madeleine*—have loved to contemplate Mary Magdalen's long retreat on the Sainte-Baume rock in Provence. These thirty years were a long dialogue of love between Christ and the one whose burning love He had accepted. While Lacordaire sees Mary Magdalen ending her life in austere penance, Bérulle contemplates her mystically associated with Christ's suffering love on the Cross, completing in her flesh, according to the words of Saint Paul, what is wanting in the sufferings of Christ for the sake of his Body the Church.

Mary Magdalen remains the one to whom was given, in an incomparable manner, an understanding of the merciful love of God manifested in the holy humanity of Jesus. In her humble, daring confidence she went straight to the Savior. Without saying a word, she spoke in the language of tears and perfume, of kisses and hair, of the body of Jesus and of her own body. She touched salvation, as did the other beneficiaries of Jesus's healings, but more than anyone else, and in a more spectacular, more daring and more unexpected way. Jesus recognised in her action the immense love of her heart. Because she was deeply sorry

48

for her sins, divine mercy carried her to the heights of mystical love, intimately associating her with the love of Jesus crucified and risen.

She is an original witness of mercy. When God's love bends down over man, plunged in the profound misery of sin, it raises him up according to a dynamic that naturally leads to the summits of love. Such indeed is the Father's mercy. It welcomes the prodigal son and fully reinstates him in his filial vocation. If he must still do penance, he will do so as a son, freely, royally, lovingly, sharing with immense love in the love of the eternal Son who freely made himself the servant of the Father's mercy.

The Innocent One

Mary Magdalen remains a model for all Christians, the majority of whom are well aware that God has much to pardon them for. It would seem that sinners are so loved by God that He gives them, rather than to those who have little or no need of forgiveness, the grace of very fervent love.

Such a hypothesis was not to the liking of little Thérèse, who, in her ardent desire to love God as much as possible, could not admit that her innocence—which a confessor had assured her of, telling her that she had never committed a mortal sin—could be an obstacle on her path of love.

This led her to express, in a particularly luminous way, an aspect of the mystery of divine mercy which one could call "prevenient mercy." It is the celebrated text called "The parable of the good doctor":

> I realised that without Him, I could have fallen as low as Saint Mary Magdalen, and the profound saying of Our Lord to Simon resonated very painfully in my soul. . . . I know that "One who is forgiven little, LOVES little" (Lk. 7:40–47), but I also know that Jesus has forgiven me more than Saint Mary Magdalen, because he has forgiven me in advance, preventing me from falling. Oh, if only I could explain what I feel! . . . Here is an example which expresses something of what I mean. Let us imagine the son of a clever doctor, coming across a stone in his path which trips him up, and, in falling, he breaks a limb; at once his father comes, picks him up lovingly, takes care of his wounds, uses all his resources and his skill and soon his son is completely cured and very grateful. Without doubt this child has good reason to love his father. But let us imagine another situation. The father, knowing that there is a stone in his son's path, hurries off in front of him and removes it, without being seen by anyone. Certainly, this child, the object of his prevenient affection, being UNAWARE of the harm from which his father has saved him, will not be grateful and will love him less than if had been healed by him . . . but if he becomes aware of the danger from which he has escaped, will he not love him

all the more? Well, I am that child, the object of
the prevenient love of a Father Who has not sent
His Word to redeem the righteous but sinners
(Mt. 9:13). He wants me to love Him not
because He has forgiven me much, but ALL
(Lk. 7:47). He did not expect me to love Him
much like Saint Mary Magdalen, but He wanted
ME to KNOW how He has loved me with an inef-
fably prevenient love, so that now I love Him like
mad. . . . I have heard it said that one does not
come across a pure soul loving more than a
repentant one, oh, how I would like to prove that
this is not true! (Ms A, 38 v° et 39 r°)

This text explains well the reasoning behind the grateful love of prevenient mercy. With remarkable sureness of
judgement, Saint Thérèse places herself in the sphere of
prevenient mercy. Far from placing herself alongside the
righteous who have no need of mercy, she knows how to
go to the root of her "righteousness," her innocence, and
understands that it is a gift of the Lord's mercy. This
understanding leads to great love, the thirst to love divine
mercy like mad. Thérèse was well aware that she ranked
among those who have experienced the Father's mercy,
and who, for that reason, can love Him more. Far from
making her puffed up, her awareness of God's prevenient
mercy kept her in her place as a creature. Small and poor,
capable of every sin if she were not prevented by grace,
she saw her innocence not as an exception setting her

apart from, or above, others, but as a perfectly normal form of divine mercy placing her, rather, below others. She is a little one, very little. She freely says, over and over again, that she is a "little soul." She abides in her nothingness, her emptiness, her littleness: "What pleases the good God in my little soul . . . is seeing me love my littleness and my poverty, the blind hope I have in his mercy. . . . That is my only treasure." (Letter 197 to Sr Marie du Sacré-Cœur, 17 September 1896)

Privileged by grace, Thérèse becomes fraternally very close to great sinners, a closeness she describes at the end of manuscript C:

> I do not make a dive for the first, but for the last place, instead of putting myself forward with the Pharisee, full of confidence, I repeat the humble prayer of the publican, but above all, I imitate Saint Mary Magdalen, her astonishing, or rather her loving boldness which delights the Heart of Jesus, captivates my heart. Yes, I feel that even if I had on my conscience all the sins that could be committed, broken-hearted with repentance I would go and throw myself into the arms of Jesus, because I know how much He cherishes the prodigal son who returns to Him. It is not because the Good God, in his prevenient mercy has preserved my soul from mortal sin that I fly to Him with confidence and love. (Ms C, 37 v°)

Thérèse describes for us the movement of her heart.

She does not rise proudly towards God, but plunges humbly and lovingly into the last place, where there is nothing but human misery embraced by the Father's mercy. She identifies herself with the publican and the Magdalen. The Innocent One identifies herself with the Sinner, thereby revealing to us that she has become a perfect spouse of the one who, being the Innocent One *par excellence,* identified himself with sinners to the point of being "made sin for us," as Saint Paul says. (2 Cor. 5:21) Mercy is God's Love identifying itself with non-love, the Good Shepherd gone in search of the lost sheep, the Son of God become a servant and bearing our sins upon himself. Thérèse teaches us that the only way to receive this mercy is to remain small, allowing merciful Love to spend itself completely.

She writes in the same letter to her sister, "Let us, then, never want to shine, let us love our littleness, let us love feeling nothing, then we shall be poor in spirit and Jesus will come looking for us, however far away we may be, and He will transform us into flames of love. . . . Oh, how I wish I could make you understand what I feel! . . . it is trust, and nothing but trust, that must lead us to Love. . . ."

A soul which, like that of Thérèse, abandons itself totally to trust and love, which places, as she says, "complete blind trust in mercy," enters into the very impulse of Love, into its dynamics. To describe this impulse, Thérèse is inspired once again by Mary Magdalen: "Just as Mary

Magdalen, constantly stooping near the empty tomb, eventually found what she is looking for, so too, I, looking down into the depths of my nothingness, could rise high enough to attain my goal." (Ms B, 3 r°–3 v°)

The movement that Thérèse describes is a living metaphor for the "movement" of divine mercy. It is an impulse which aims at the lowest point and springs from there to the loftiest. Coming forth from the Eternal Father's Heart, it strides like a giant towards the most wretched of sinners in order to return, with him, to the inaccessible heights of the Father's eternal Love.

Like the Sinner, the Innocent One descends ever lower and lower in her smallness, her poverty, her nothingness. She faithfully espouses the descending curve of humility. At the same time, she never ceases to fly towards Jesus with a daring that is full of love; in him she touches both the nothingness of the creature and the loftiness of the Creator.

Mary Immaculate

The Sinner and the Innocent One have, as it were, taken us by the hand and led us quite naturally to Mary Immaculate. Our Lady's Immaculate Conception is the masterpiece of prevenient mercy, the summit of the "mercy stairway."

Like the Sinner—and even more so—the Immaculate Virgin, ever unacquainted with tears of repentance, has nevertheless been washed in the Blood of Christ. She has been projected by mercy towards the summits of Love, and of merciful Love.

Like the Innocent One—and even more so—the Immaculate Virgin identifies herself with the dynamism of mercy, with that movement of God towards man, towards the smallest, the poorest, the most sinful.

From Our Lady to Mary Magdalen and Thérèse there is thus an irresistible attraction: that of souls united by the mercy of the Living God.

Our Lady and Mary Magdalen lived in close proximity with one another. Both were, at least in part, companions of Jesus's public life. There is no doubt that the Son's special love for Mary Magdalen found an echo in Mary's heart. The All-Pure felt herself to be very much the sister of the one who had been the Great Sinner. Filled with the same mystery of mercy, both ran together along the ways of Love. Our Lady's role was higher, more hidden, more silent. That of Mary Magdalen was more visible. Mary Magdalen was more out of the ordinary, Our Lady more universal.

There is nothing surprising about finding these two women together where it all springs from, nearest to the pierced Heart. Thoroughly united in their loving compassion, they are nevertheless clearly distinct from one another. Mary is the Mother of Jesus. She is confirmed and consecrated as Mother of the members of the Body of Christ, Mother of the believer, Mother of the Church. She is clearly seen to hold the first place. She is the first in the order of mercy received, the first of the redeemed, the first of the forgiven. She is the Mother of all those souls who receive mercy. She is the Mother of the Sinner and of the Innocent One.

Here the meaning of her privilege shines out. Mary Immaculate has been called to a universal motherhood in the Spirit according to the order of the Father's merciful grace. She is the Queen of Mercy. This is right and fitting, for she is, and remains, the Mother of Mercy Incarnate in her Son Jesus. *Regina misericordiæ, mater misericordiæ*, Queen of Mercy, Mother of Mercy, as we sing in the *Salve Regina*.

For all poor sinners, Mary Immaculate is a most loving sister, but above all she is a Mother full of mercy. Every grace of forgiveness comes to us through her. Mary Immaculate is truly close to the sinner, especially to the greatest sinner, and this is not just a matter of sentimentalism flowing from the fact that she is a maternal figure. Her Immaculate Conception itself places the Blessed Virgin at the head of the order of mercy. Her sinful brothers and sisters have been confided to her in a very special way, one that is properly maternal.

So it is no surprise that Thérèse, however near she was to Mary Magdalen, would be even closer to Our Lady. It would be easy to demonstrate this. The audacity of Thérèse's love goes as far as a kind of exchange with Our Lady, ingeniously expressed in this little note: "Oh Mary, if you were Thérèse and I were the Queen of Heaven, I would like to be Thérèse so that you could be the Queen of Heaven." Thérèse has perfectly understood Mary Immaculate's maternal heart and given expression to it. As Mother, and however near to us the Saints, our brothers and sisters, may be, Mary has a uniquely privileged place of proximity to us.

In the end, the Sinner, the Innocent One, and Mary Immaculate merge in the rays of the manifold glory of the merciful and most Holy Trinity. By their example, by their sisterly presence, by their maternal attention, which reaches its perfection in Our Lady, they draw and guide the poor sinners that we all are towards the Father of mercy. The privilege of her Immaculate Conception places Mary among the finest achievements of the grace of salvation among human beings, the one closest to God, but for that very reason—Mary Magdalen and Thérèse help us to understand this better—as the one who is also closest to men.

IV

The Mirror and
the Flaming Torch

A S THE HEARTS OF BELIEVERS HAVE ALWAYS understood, the All-Pure is also the Nearest. The
period of history which immediately preceded
and followed the definition of the dogma of the Immaculate Conception by Blessed Pius IX on the 8th of December, 1854, saw important signs of Our Lady's presence
flourish in the life of the Church.

There were, first of all, the apparitions of the Rue du
Bac in 1830, which resulted in the spread of the miraculous medal and its invocation: "O Mary, conceived without sin, pray for us who have recourse to you." Catherine
Labouré (1806–1876) benefited from three apparitions of
the Virgin in 1830: on 18 July, 27 November and an
unspecified date in December. It was during the second of
these apparitions that she saw a picture representing Mary
Immaculate and received instructions to have a medal like
it struck. The appearance of the Blessed Virgin was
accompanied by a promise of graces, symbolised by the
rays streaming from Our Lady's hands. Mary Immaculate
revealed herself as radiant with the gifts of God.

Twelve years later, on the 20th of January, 1842, a zealous Jew accompanied a friend of his for a few minutes into the church of S. Andrea delle Fratte in Rome. A few days earlier, this friend had urged him to agree to wear a miraculous medal, which he did with profound skepticism. Alphonse Ratisbonne (1814–1884) recounted shortly afterwards:

> I had only been inside the church for a moment when suddenly I felt seized by a distress I cannot put into words. I raised my eyes: the whole building seemed to have disappeared from my sight, all the light was focused, so to speak, on a single chapel, and amidst all this brightness there appeared standing on the altar, large, shining, full of majesty and sweetness, the Virgin Mary, just as she is on my medal; an irresistible force drove me towards her. With her hand the Virgin made me a sign to kneel down, she seemed to say to me: "It is all right." She did not speak to me, but I understood everything.

Ten days later, Alphonse Ratisbonne received Baptism, Confirmation and the Eucharist. With his brother Père Théodard, himself a convert to Catholicism several years earlier, he would found the congregation of Our Lady of Sion for the conversion of the Jewish people.

In 1858, at Lourdes, in the heart of the Pyrenees, an illiterate young shepherd girl went looking for dry wood near the grotto of Massabielle, on the bank of the Gave. When she was preparing to cross it, a gust of wind caught her attention. In the cleft of the rock she saw "something white in the shape of a lady." The encounter, begun on 11 February, would continue. On February 14, the beautiful Lady gladly welcomed being sprinkled with holy water, and her fingers followed the rosary that Bernadette Soubirous (1844–1879) recited. On her third visit, the Lady asked Bernadette, "Would you be so kind as to come here for 15 days?" These days would be the fortnight of apparitions from 18 February to 4 March 1858. On 24 February, the Virgin pronounced the word, "Penance!" Then she added: "Pray for the conversion of sinners." She asked Bernadette to "Go and kiss the ground in reparation for sinners." On Thursday the 25th came the command to drink from the spring and to wash there, to kiss the ground, to drink the water, to wash in it, to eat the grass. On 2 March, the lady asked for a chapel to be built and a for a great procession.

Then, after an interruption in the encounters, Bernadette felt impelled to go to the grotto again in the early hours of 25 March, feast of the Annunciation. After reciting the rosary in front of the Lady, she again asked her three times the question, "Please *Mademoiselle*, would you be so kind as to tell me who you are?" Three times, her question obtained only smiles. The fourth time, the Lady opened her joined hands and stretched them earthwards. Then she joined them in front of her breast, raised her eyes to heaven and said: "*Que soy era Immaculada Councepciou.*" "I am the Immaculate Conception." We know what followed: how Bernadette ran to the presbytery, how the parish priest Père Peyramale was deeply moved, how the last apparition occurred on Easter Wednesday, 7 April, how official recognition followed on 18 January 1862, and how, during all this time, crowds flocked to Lourdes in an uninterrupted and ever-increasing flow.

The spread of a medal, the conversion of a young aristocrat and the flow of sick and sinners drawn towards the Grotto at Lourdes constitute many tangible signs of the active presence of Mary Immaculate. The dogmatic declaration of 8 December 1854 cannot be reduced to the conclusion of a long enquiry which only concerned theologians. The Immaculate Conception is certainly a speculative truth, an abstract affirmation on one of the mysteries of our faith. Yet it imposes itself on the life of the Christian as a living reality, the active and efficacious presence in the very heart of the Church's history of the unique woman who was Jesus's Mother.

Two saints can help us examine this presence. Though superficially very different from one another, Bernadette and Maximilian Kolbe are both privileged witnesses of Mary Immaculate in our time.

Bernadette, Mirror of Mary Immaculate

Bernadette ran to her parish priest's house. All the way there, she kept repeating the words she had received from the Lady. What did they mean? She had no idea. She kept repeating them precisely because she was afraid of forgetting them. She knew absolutely nothing about the dogma of the Immaculate Conception of Our Lady. The words "Trinity" or "transubstantiation" meant nothing to her. It was only after the apparitions that she would make her First Holy Communion, not having done particularly well at her catechism lessons for want of a good memory. All her life, when she evoked the scene, she would have difficulty pronouncing or writing properly the Patois or French terms for the Immaculate Conception. She habitually spoke neither of Mary Immaculate nor of the Immaculate Virgin, but simply of the "Holy Virgin."

However surprising this fact might seem at first, Bernadette's spiritual life was not centered on the Immaculate Conception. It would be left to others to develop the consequences of the way Our Lady of Lourdes defined herself.

On the other hand, Bernadette lived in the immediate radiance of Mary Immaculate and bore invaluable witness to her. If, in the numerous interrogations she underwent, Bernadette impressed those who questioned her by her tranquillity, her openness, her precision, and her luminous sincerity, it may be said that she literally fascinated them when she repeated for them the gestures and attitudes which had accompanied the manifestation of that name. The most severe interrogators literally "melted" in the face of such authenticity.

All her life, Bernadette would make the sign of the Cross as Our Lady had taught her to do in her vision. In her entire person, as in her gestures, Bernadette is a kind of mirror of Mary Immaculate. Because she was loved by Our Lady, she received a vivid impression in her soul, and in her entire being, of the one she had encountered in an entirely unique way.

Like Mary, Bernadette is small, in physical stature as well as in social standing. Straightaway she places herself among the poor, and the last of these. She is a sister to all who are small and poor in any way, the sick, the infirm, sinners.

Like Mary, Bernadette is unfailingly obedient: to the Spirit Who guides her interiorly, to the Blessed Virgin who shows her gestures of penance, to the Church, whom she recognized in the members of the hierarchy and, later, in her religious superiors.

Like Mary, Bernadette walks along the path of faith, accepting severe moral and physical trials, entering lovingly into the mystery of the Savior's Cross.

Like Mary, Bernadette extended mercy to all, especially to the sick and the suffering. She entered the Sisters of Nevers out of a desire to care for the sick.

Like Mary, Bernadette plunged herself into the mystery of the hidden life, consisting of silence, sacrifice, prayer and the gift of self, of suffering and of powerlessness. She made the furrow of humility ever deeper. Sickness reduced her to nothing, to being virtually unable to do anything; she acquiesced entirely, with that playful simplicity which was a special charm of hers.

The grace of childhood emanated from Bernadette's entire person. How can we not see in this a reflection of the eternal youthfulness of Mary Immaculate? The handmaid reflects in herself the face of the Queen she serves. She unites herself with the humility of Mary's *Fiat*. She abides in her poverty, in her emptiness, in her utter lowliness.

Thus Bernadette, mirror of Mary Immaculate, seems to tell us that Mary herself is a mirror, the perfectly pure mirror of the glory of the Word Incarnate. In the humble visionary of Lourdes is reflected the light of Mary Immaculate, who is herself the pure image of her Son, the Suffering Servant, poor and humble, radiating the Father's mercy.

By her life in the luminous shadow of Mary Immaculate, Bernadette enables us to touch Christ and to let ourselves be touched by his merciful closeness. She thus reveals to us those aspects of the presence of Mary Immaculate to which our hearts are most sensitive. Bernadette's special gift is that of complete simplicity, poverty, emptiness. She makes no great discourses, performs no outstanding actions; on the contrary, she plunges herself ever more deeply into the most profound humility. In this way, she constantly shows us the empty space within ourselves where grace can reach, expand, and eventually shine forth. All beauty belongs to Mary and to Christ. Bernadette manages to attract us by disappearing into a shadow in her own eyes and striving to disappear as far as possible in the eyes of the world. She who was so radiant and celestial during the apparitional ecstasies, she who was still so full of light when bearing witness and when patiently recounting what had happened to her, resolutely chose the shade and reserve. And in this self-effacement, she is quietly all-present.

Maximilian Kolbe, Flaming Torch of Mary Immaculate

In complete contrast to Saint Bernadette, Saint Maximilian Kolbe (1894–1941) was fascinated by the name revealed by the Lady in the grotto. He saw more in this title than a simple name or appellation. He understood these words as stating Mary's most profound identity; a paradoxical identity, because who but God defines himself in abstract terms? Father Peyramele had already said, "A lady cannot have that name! You are mistaken! Do you know what that means?" And each one would correct it in their own way: "I am the Immaculate Virgin," or "Mary Immaculate," or "the Virgin of the Immaculate Conception." For Father Kolbe, the formula was like lightning. Mary says who she is. He would spend the rest of his life striving to understand, and enable others to understand, this revolutionary message, and to draw from it its missionary consequences.

First of all, Father Kolbe constantly fathomed the mystery of Mary's name. "Who are you, O Immaculate Conception?" he would repeat in all kinds of circumstances.

Through an intuition proper to him, Saint Maximilian would discover a very special affinity between Mary and the Holy Spirit. In the mystery of the Holy Trinity, he contemplated the Father, Who is the One Who engenders, and the Son, Who is the Engendered One. Then he considered the Spirit. The third Person "is the fruit of the Love of the Father and of the Son. The fruit of created love is a created conception [the child]. But the fruit of Love, the prototype of this created love, is itself necessarily conception. The Spirit is thus the uncreated, eternal Conception, the prototype of every conception in the universe. [...] The Spirit is thus this most holy, infinitely holy, immaculate Conception." (Sketch, 17-2-41, quoted by H.M. Manteau-Bonamy, O.P., *La doctrine mariale du Père Kolbe,* Lethielleux, Paris, 1975, 28–31)

The Virgin Mary is the most perfect spouse of this Spirit, Who is Immaculate Conception. She has been created in the Spirit, that is to say, united to him in an inseparable way. She is entirely moulded by the Holy Spirit, totally given over to the Love with which God loves Himself. She is Immaculate because, being without sin from the very origin of her being, she is entirely open to the action of the Spirit and, above all, to his Person. The Father and the Son conceive the Holy Spirit, the immaculate fruit of their love, in her. The Spirit allows himself to be conceived in her Immaculate Heart.

The Most Holy Spirit lives in the soul of Mary Immaculate, in her very being, He makes her fruitful, and that from the very first moment of her existence, throughout her entire life and on into eternity. [...] In the Holy Spirit's union with her, it is not just a question of the love of two beings, but in one of them it is the entire love of the Holy Trinity, and in the other it is the entire love of creation, and thus in this union heaven is united with the earth, the whole of heaven is united with the whole of the earth, eternal love in its entirety with created love in its entirety. This is the summit of love. [...] If among creatures, the bride takes the bridegroom's name because she belongs to him, is one with him, becomes his equal and with him is a creative principal of life, how much more is the Holy Spirit's name: Immaculate Conception, the name of her in whom He lives as Love, principal of life in the entire supernatural order of grace. (Ibid.)

In the name Mary gives to Bernadette, Father Kolbe discovers a revelation of the intimate bond which unites the Virgin and the Holy Spirit. In certain daring texts, he goes as far as saying that Mary is a kind of "incarnation" of the Holy Spirit. Whatever expressions he uses, he wants them to be even stronger, shedding full light of the union of Mary and the Spirit wherein he sees the origin of the incomparable role of Mary Immaculate in the plan of universal salvation as well as in the life of every human being.

Because Mary Immaculate is so closely linked to the Spirit, the more we belong to her, the more also we belong to the Holy Spirit, and the more the divine life grows and blossoms in us. Father Kolbe, with consuming zeal, therefore encourages consecration to Mary Immaculate. This is not a matter of an exterior act, but a commitment understood as extending to the whole person—that of giving oneself to Mary Immaculate in order to really belong to her, to live with her, to be one with her, and thus, in the end, to be one with Christ and with the Triune God. In his extension of Saint Louis-Marie Grignion de Montfort's consecration to Mary, Saint Maximilian Kolbe urges all Christians to give themselves to Mary: "I humbly implore you to accept my entire being as your goods and your property, and to act in me and in all the faculties of my soul and of my body, in my entire life, my death and my eternity, just as you please."

At a first reading, we will perhaps be shocked by such strong expressions. However, Father Kolbe is aiming after all at the total gift of each person to God Himself. But how are we to give ourselves to God except by the hands of the very one through whom God gave Himself to us? Moreover, it is not so much a question of putting pressure on Mary by consecrating oneself to her, as of consenting to her prevenient action. For, as at Lourdes or the Rue du Bac, Mary Immaculate appears before souls on Earth, offering herself to them. She draws them into the graces radiating around her. She is the maternal climate in which the Holy Spirit offers himself to men's hearts in order to become himself their holiness, to create in them the most perfect adherence to the will of God, the most complete response of love.

In this certitude, Maximilian Kolbe had no fear of the loftiest ambitions—the hope, no less, of consecrating the whole world to Mary Immaculate so that, by her, the entire created universe might be handed over to Christ. For this purpose, the apostle of the Immaculate founded, in 1917, the *Militia Immaculatæ*, called "The Militia of the Immaculate" in English. It grew considerably during his lifetime. In the spirit of Father Kolbe, this institution counteracted the more or less secret movements such as Freemasonry, of whose harmful influence the saint had become aware during his studies in Rome. Seen in this way, the presence of Mary Immaculate is not reduced to an action in the private sphere of personal devotion. Instead, it sets in motion all the supernatural resources of salvation in order to penetrate into every domain of human life, the family, society, economics, politics and culture, by means of men and women who are totally consecrated to Mary Immaculate, and as such, acting as humble and efficacious instruments of the Spirit working for the salvation of men.

With Father Kolbe, contemplating Mary in her Immaculate Conception seems to reach a summit. It was not enough for him to admire the infinite purity of the Virgin of Nazareth, nor could imitating her virtues and making the attitudes of her soul his own satisfy him. His loving gaze upon Mary had to lead to an identification with her. To become one with her, to belong to her, would be to allow her to take possession of our being in a divine and maternal way. Thus, God Himself wishes to transform us into Himself, to divinize us, to make us "holy and immaculate before Him in love." (Eph. 1:4) Therefore, Mary Immaculate is "completely divine"—not because she is God, but because nothing in her belongs to her, but all belongs to the Spirit. Father Kolbe writes: "Truly, we are very weak, and very often we feel this weakness, but the only way forward is our consecration to Mary Immaculate." (Conference of 9 March 1940, Manteau-Bonamy, 123)

And again: "We must entrust ourselves to Mary Immaculate, she is completely divine. We must divest ourselves of self as fast as we can, and keep nothing back for ourselves, absolutely nothing: it must be she who does everything." (Conference of 17 February 1938, ibid.)

In the end, the example of Bernadette and the message of Father Kolbe coincide perfectly. She who is the utterly Pure one, is also the utterly Poor one. Mary Immaculate attracts all souls in the realism of the first beatitude: "Blessed are the poor in spirit." (Mt. 5:3) It is as one who is poor that a creature enters into the divine life: poverty of external goods, certainly, but more than that, a poverty inscribed in one's being. Radical dispossession and the entire gift of self can enable every believer to become a mirror and a burning torch of Mary Immaculate. It is these that render a soul as transparent as pure water, utterly penetrated with the Light of God, wherein is already reflected the divine beauty of the Face of Mary Immaculate, our Sister and our Mother.

V

O Mary, Conceived
Without Sin, Pray For Us!

"O MARY, CONCEIVED WITHOUT SIN, PRAY FOR US who have recourse to thee." This inscription on the miraculous medal teaches us to pray to Mary Immaculate. Indeed, Mary Immaculate prays for us. She intercedes for the poor sinners who whisper her name in their hearts and on their lips while they recite the Rosary: "Holy Mary, Mother of God, pray for us sinners." Mary, the Immaculate one, intercedes for us as she shares in the fullness of life of the resurrection of her Son in the glory of her Assumption. She prays to Jesus for us. She turns to our High Priest, through whom we "draw near to God," "since he always lives to make intercession" for us, as the Letter to the Hebrews teaches us. (7:25) She does so now because she has always done so. She intercedes in heaven as she did on earth.

Mystery of Mercy

A meditation upon Mary's intercession may begin at Cana. The narrative of the wedding at Cana provides us with the first mention of Mary (out of only two!) in Saint John's Gospel. The wedding feast is a time of profound human joy with a deeply symbolic meaning. It is a sign, a sacrament of the nuptial relationship between God and his people: God and Israel, but also Christ and the Church, according to Saint Paul: "Husbands, love your wives, as Christ loved the church and gave himself up for her . . . that he may present the church to himself in splendor, without spot or wrinkle, . . . holy and without blemish." (Eph. 6:25–27) Christ gave himself up for the Church in order that she might become Immaculate.

As always, the handmaid of the Lord is not at the top table, but next to the servants. From there, she sees the practical aspects of the feast. She sees the need, she understands the trouble, and she acts without delay. She does not search for any human expedient. She goes directly to her Son and expresses the need to him: "They have no wine." When Mary sees our needs—or when we speak to her of them—she turns immediately to Jesus. She puts the needs of mankind in the midst of the relationship between Jesus and herself.

We know Jesus's answer. It seems, at first sight, disrespectful towards his mother: "O woman, what have you to do with me?" (RSV) or, closer to the Greek text, "O, woman, what is this to thee and me?" The statement has a tone of reproach, as Jesus begins by acknowledging that his mother has put things between them. Jesus knows that he cannot refuse his mother anything, not only because of their mutual affection, but also because Mary has never refused him anything. Jesus is sensitive to

Mary's request more than to any other. He cannot resist her request, which implicitly asks him to engage himself completely in his answer. But why is she so eager to see him intervene?

It cannot be that Jesus does not care for our earthly needs. Yet he seems to wonder: Is it time for him to act? In his answer, Jesus refers to the core of his mission: "My hour has not yet come." In the fourth Gospel, the hour signifies the time of Jesus's exaltation on the cross, when he fully accomplishes the revelation of the Father. His hour is the time of his full obedience to the Father. It is the time when he reveals to the world the Father's mercy, his readiness to forgive, his unlimited grace. Every grace comes from the Cross of Jesus. Any intercession made by Jesus depends on his hour. His glorious Passion is the main work of God's grace through Jesus. In it, the favor of the Father for the world, his love and his grace, are perfectly manifested. The basis of any answered prayer is Jesus's exaltation on the cross.

As his answer to Mary shows, Jesus himself waits for his hour. He does not anticipate the time of God, the time of his Father. God answers human requests in due time. In the "fullness of time," when the time is full of His love, He gives His Son up for us. This is the source of any answer to our petitions, according to Saint Paul: "He who did not spare his own Son, but gave him up for us all, will he not also give us all things with him?" (Rom. 8:32) Any request we make to Jesus through Mary is directed towards the mercy of the Father, who mercifully gives his Son for the world (Jn. 3:16) "when the time" has "fully come." (Ga. 4:4)

As Mary turned to her Son, Jesus now turns to his Father, as he does in all circumstances. The Father's mercy is the source of any answer to our prayers. The merciful Father is the "throne of grace" from which, according to the Letter to the Hebrews, we "receive mercy and find grace to help in time of need." (4:16) When we pray to Mary and she prays to Jesus, our petition reaches the Father Himself. He is the "Father of lights" from whom "every good endowment and every perfect gift" comes. (Jm. 1:17) He "gives to all men generously and without reproaching." (Jm. 1:5) In His mercy, He is the one source of all gifts.

In the dialogue between Mary and Jesus, our requests are presented to the Father's mercy. Mary's privilege as the Immaculate One establishes her in utter dependence on the redeeming sacrifice of the Son on the Cross and on the mercy of the Father. When she prays to Jesus, she is ultimately asking for Jesus's blood, which made her what she is. In this sacrifice, the full mercy of the Father was revealed and opened to sinners. She can exclaim with Saint Paul: "The saying is sure and worthy of full acceptance, that Christ Jesus came into the world to save sinners. And I am the foremost of sinners; but I received mercy for this reason, that in me, as the foremost, Jesus Christ might display his perfect patience as an example to those who believe in him for eternal life." (1 Tim. 1:15–16) The perfectly pure one, to whom mercy was given as a preservation of sin, is the advocate of mercy. She proclaims the mercy of the Lord and intercedes directly and powerfully with the source of mercy: the sacrifice of her Son in which the merciful designs of the Father are accomplished and revealed.

The Immaculate one prays to the Father through Jesus as a perfect mirror of His mercy. She prays for us in the simplest way: she presents us and all our needs through Jesus to the light of God's mercy. When we pray to Mary as poor sinners, she puts us and all our needs in the light of the Father's mercy. Mary intercedes for us because she goes further than anyone else into the mystery of the Father's mercy. Indeed, she benefitted from it more than all of us, but also for all of us. Her privilege entitles her to call upon God's mercy for us. The Immaculate is, as such, entitled to intercede with the Father through Jesus and together with Jesus. Indeed, this intercession is part of her mission as Immaculate Mother of God. All the power of her intercession comes from her privilege. According to Tradition, she is "*omnipotentia supplex*," the one who is all-powerful in her intercession. She is so because she spontaneously receives her own being and everything that she has from the mercy of the Father, manifested in the loving sacrifice of the Son.

Mystery of Obedience

In a second movement, after she has prayed to her Son, Mary turns to us. She invites us to obey Jesus: "Do whatever he tells you." She draws us into the mystery of obedience which is at the core of the hour of Jesus. She is fully consecrated to this mystery, as she says to the Angel at the Annunciation: "Let it be to me according to your word." (Lk. 1:38) Just as Jesus obeys the Father, Mary obeys her Son and invites us to do the same.

What is obeying? It is partaking in God's work. Jesus is at work; the Son is always working, as the Father is always working. (Jn. 5:17) Their work is to give life. At the beginning of the world, we call it creation. Providence and government of the world include the subsequent steps of revelation and salvation and culminate in the glorification or deification of the redeemed world, already begun in Jesus's Ascension and Mary's Assumption, and still to be fully realized in us all. Although we need, as creatures existing in time, to distinguish all these different aspects, there is obviously only one work of God. The whole drama of the world is one divine gift of life. History exists only from the perspective of those who receive the divine gift—and all divine gifts in which the one divine gift unfolds in time—allowing us to respond freely to this gift.

By faith, human beings welcome this gift and respond to it by giving themselves back to God. By faith, man works with God. We partake by faith and obedience in the mystery of God's work in the world. This is what Mary did at the Annunciation: she believed and obeyed, she trusted and acted. We too work together with God when we believe and when, in faith, hope and love, we offer all that we are and all that we do to His Holy Spirit: "This is the true work of God that you believe in him whom He has sent." (Jn. 6:29)

Obedience is the work of faith. Faith gives us light; it makes us understand God's will, so that we do not obey like slaves, but like sons who relate to their Father. Through the Son whom he sent into the world to accomplish his will of salvation, and through the sacramental actions of the Church, we are in direct relationship with our Father. We believe in the Father, who has sent His Son and given His Spirit of Truth, and we obey Him.

Thus it happens that to trust in the word of Christ and to obey his commandments are one and the same thing, which we call faith or obedience. Saint Paul speaks of "the obedience of faith." (Rom. 1:5) And John gives a summary of the new commandment with these words: "This is his commandment, that we should believe in the name of his Son Jesus Christ and love one another, just as he has commanded us." (1 Jn. 3:23)

Well-prepared by Mary and following her advice, we are ready to listen to Jesus's command: "Fill the jars with water."

Our prayers are not answered by a sign coming from above, for which we should only wait in the most passive way, as if *God* does everything and *we* simply look and wait. Nor does the answer come only from us, as if, once we have expressed to God our needs, He simply gives us His blessing to do what is to be done, as if we simply do everything under God's gaze. The truth is that *God-with-us* works with and within our obedient faith. While we are filling the jars, he is making the wine. Our obedient faith works together with his loving mercy. It is fascinating to note that the text about Cana contains no account of the miracle in itself. It does not report that Jesus said anything or did anything to affect the water in the jars. John tells us only that when the water was brought to the steward of the feast, it had become wine, and an excellent wine at that! When God gives an order, He works with us and is doing His work within our participation. According to Blaise Pascal, we have to "do little things as though they were great, because of the majesty of Jesus Christ who does them in us, and who lives our life; we have to do great things as though they were small and easy, because of his omnipotence." (*The Thoughts*, Mystery of Jesus)

The words of Mary, "Do whatever he tells you," are the fruit of Mary's experience of faith. She not only trusts Jesus utterly, but knows how to work with him and under his guidance. When we pray to Mary, she teaches us the active prayer of obedient faith which is hers. We are taught by her how to work with God in faith and obedience in the smallest things of daily life. The jars waiting to be filled are a powerful symbol of Christian life. We pour water day after day; we give our lives, day in and day out, and Jesus makes of them the wine of his marriage feast with us. From the old rites, Jesus creates the new sacrament. From the things of the earth, he gives divine realities. From the small gifts we are able to offer with his grace, he works marvels. These marvels are not necessarily miracles which we might be able to observe. Rather, they are generally the deep and invisible action of God in the world, the mystery of His work, in which every single human action can be integrated, as a part, into a whole which God alone knows. Thirty years of hidden life gave to Mary a real expertise in the obscure and faithful way through which we are invited to work together with God. These thirty years were for her years of obedient faith which prepared her to take part in Jesus's main act of obedience and to stand at the foot of the cross in the most active compassion. There, she suffered and offered herself together with Jesus, united with him in a perfect "Yes" to the Father.

Just as Jesus in heaven intercedes for us by presenting to the Father the sacrifice of his perfect obedience which led him to give himself up for us, so Mary presents to Jesus her perfect obedience as handmaid of the Lord and mother of men. The intercession of Jesus and Mary is one and the same obedience to the Father. In Jesus, this obedience is totally received from the Father. In Mary, it is totally received from Jesus. Both intercede for us as poor ones.

Mystery of Poverty

Obviously, Mary knows that everything, in her faith and obedience, is the gift of God and, more precisely, a fruit of the Redemption accomplished by her Son. When she presents her obedience to Jesus, she gives him what she received from him. She intercedes for us as the poor one *par excellence.* Her intercession does not add anything to the intercession of Jesus; it only expresses the thanksgiving and grateful praise of a poor creature loved by God. Mary intercedes for us as a pure reflection of Jesus's perfect love for us men.

In the perfect mirror which the Immaculate is, we are given a glimpse of the poverty of the Son. Just as Mary receives everything from her Son, even her power of intercession, so the Son receives all that he is from the Father. In the outpouring of himself for us in the mystery of Redemption, the Son opens to us all the riches of the Divine Love which he gives to us. At the same time, he gives to the Father the perfect glory of his Love by giving himself up utterly to the will of the Father, to his loving design of salvation through death and resurrection: "Father, the hour has come, glorify thy Son that the Son may glorify thee." (Jn. 17:1) God is perfectly rich and possesses Himself and all things perfectly. At the same time, he is perfectly poor, because he constantly gives all that he is in an exchange of love and glory which is the life of the Holy Trinity. In Jesus's intercession, the poverty of the Son meets the poverty of the Father in their common

Spirit, who is "*Pater pauperum*," the Father of the Poor, the Person in whom the perfect poverty of God's love is manifested.

Mary, full of grace and Spouse of the Spirit, is the one who enters most deeply into her Son's poverty. She mirrors Jesus's poverty in her being, and she follows the poor Jesus in her life. At the hour of the *kenosis*, Mary stands at the foot of the cross, letting herself be transformed by the sacrifice of her Son. She becomes the mother of the faithful, who are all represented by the beloved disciple. She is deprived of her Son, who is handed over and who hands himself up. At the same time, she receives a new son. As a Mother, she sees her maternity broadened as she welcomes in the disciple, the type of all those who share in the mystery of her Son. Her mission is to help them become children of God (Jn. 1:12), to live fully in the Spirit of her Son.

Mystery of Love

"On the third day there was a marriage at Cana in Galilee, and the mother of Jesus was there." (Jn. 2:1) The marriage feast on the third day provides the context for Mary's intercession. The third day is the eschatological day of salvation, when the spiritual Isaac is offered to the Father and given back in his resurrection. (cf. Heb. 11:18–19) It is the day of the mystical marriage between God and man, in which the mystery of Incarnation is fulfilled. Jesus is the bridegroom (Jn. 3:29) who presents his beloved Bride, the Church, with the chalice of his blood in which she is purified and made worthy of being his Spouse.

The Immaculate anticipates this mystery in her very being, as she is, from the first moment of her conception, in complete harmony of will and beauty with the Redeemer. She thus becomes perfectly associated with the work of Redemption, the one who always works together with Jesus, who perfectly shares his Spirit.

Mary's intercession is a mystery of love in which Jesus and Mary, the Bridegroom and the Bride, Christ and the Church, are perfectly one in love. In her Immaculate Heart is perfectly realised the mystery of the intercession of the Spirit himself who, according to Saint Paul, "intercedes for the saints according to the will of God." (Rom. 8:26) Intercession is ultimately a mystery of love in the Holy Spirit. Here we do not encounter the image of a hard Father somehow made more pleasant by the generous intervention of His Son, the latter being himself persuaded, as it were, to stand for men by a good mother who places herself between him and us. On the contrary, the Immaculate's intercession reveals to us the mystery of grace, which springs out of the wise designs of the loving and merciful Father, and is accomplished in the gift which the Son makes of himself for the world out of love for the Father (Jn. 14:31) in perfect union with the Father's love for the world. (Jn. 3:16) Mary, full of grace from the very beginning of her life, benefits to the full from that grace.

In return, she puts herself wholly at the service of the economy of grace and finds her place, as Mother, in the dispensation of grace. In her, the efficacious intercession of the Church finds its model and its maternal source.

Mary intercedes for us more than any other saint because she gave herself totally to the mercy of the Father, to the obedience of the Son and to the poverty of the Spirit. In love, she is one with Jesus in his prayer to the Father for all who believe in him. Jesus receives from her all that he presents to the Father. In return, she puts all that she received from him at his service alone. By her Immaculate Conception, she is totally dedicated to the mission of her Son which she makes her own in loving obedience to the Father's designs. Spouse of the Spirit, she intercedes in him and with him, within the mystery of Love eternal which saves us.

As we pray to Mary Immaculate, we learn from her the qualities that make for good intercession: her poverty, her obedience, her confidence in God's mercy, and her union in love with Jesus. As we pray to Mary, she makes of us intercessors, with her and in her, in communion with her Son and in Him. She gives us a share in the movement of grace that goes out from the Father as a gift and comes back to Him as an intercession. This merciful gift of love, which can only be received in utter poverty, calls for an obedience that is full of trust in God, whose merciful designs are mysteriously accomplished in our lives. There exists only one prayer: that of the Spirit in the Heart of

Jesus and in the hearts of all those whom he deigns to call his brothers and sisters. Mary Immaculate is the very first among them.

VI

The Sacred Heart
of Jesus
and The Immaculate Heart
of Mary

Cor ad cor loquitur. HEART SPEAKS UNTO HEART. BL. JOHN Henry Newman's famous motto finds its perfect realization in Jesus and Mary. Between the Sacred Heart of Jesus and the Immaculate Heart of Mary, there is a constant exchange in which the Word is spoken and the Spirit given.

Jesus, as any child, receives his mother's love. Her Heart speaks, *loquitur,* first. From her heart, filled with the fullness of the Spirit, the *kecharitomene,* the "full of grace," pours love into her Son's Heart. She loves and gives him human life. She loves and nourishes his life. She loves and shelters his life.

In this action, Mary experiences genuine spiritual joy. In giving to her Son, she actually gives to God Himself. She does so as a poor woman who knows that she does not possess anything, that she has received all that she has and all that she is. And it is precisely her joy to be able to give "out of her poverty" to her Son his humanity as son of man, and her motherly love, the complete homage of her maternal Heart, "everything she had, her whole living." (cf. Mk. 12:44)

Jesus, too, is a poor man who receives with gratitude. The Incarnate Word, "though he was rich, yet for [our] sake became poor, so that by his poverty [we] might become rich." (2 Cor. 8:9) He reveals himself as "gentle and lowly in heart." He receives with wonder. Very often, in the Gospel, we see Jesus admiring the faith, the generosity, or the humility of people He encounters, especially women. He must have wondered with the same gratitude at his mother's love. As any loved child, he experienced his mother's love as inexhaustible, unlimited, and, in some sense, infinite. There is much place, he knew, in Mary's Heart. She could, for sure, welcome the beloved disciple as her son, and through him, all of us. The poor Jesus, in the supreme poverty of the cross, draws the whole world into Mary's loving Heart. The world he so loved, he gives to his loving mother, whose presence at the foot of the cross fills him with love.

In her Son's heart, Mary's love encounters its source. The Mother of the Son is also the disciple of the Word. Her love is always an answer to Jesus who, from the very first moment, is wholly Word, loving revelation, Jesus who *loquitur*, who speaks the first. It is the privilege of the Mother as first disciple to gaze, beyond the words, in silence and in love, into Jesus's Heart. The *Verbum infans,* the silent Word, is full of the loving knowledge of his

Father, and Mary receives all that her Son reveals to her. By his presence and by the very gift that he is as her Son, he expresses above all one thing, the "one necessary": his Father. This single Word—*Abba,* Father—is expressed in the many words and events of Jesus's life and teaching. Mary welcomes all these "things" which God has hidden from "the wise and understanding and revealed to babes." She makes herself fully a disciple of her Son, who reveals to her the Father. She is an ear perfectly listening to God's Word. She answers it by the perfect homage of her faith, by her loving discipleship.

Moreover, in her Immaculate Heart, she keeps all the deeds and words of her Son. Her Heart is a loving memory in which things past are welcomed and stored. These memories can be drawn out when necessary and seen again in the light of new events and new *words.* The always-refreshing light of the Holy Spirit does not cease to reveal to her new aspects of the eternal mystery of love.

The two holy Hearts are in constant dialogue and perfect harmony. The same truth and the same love fill them both; an unceasing communication of light and love exists between them. The fruit of this exchange is the Holy Spirit. The Spirit of Love is the living and personal unity of the two Sacred Hearts. They are one in him. They look together, as it were, in the direction of the Spirit, the "First Gift" in whom each of them receives the other and experiences his or her self as a gift to the other, a gift for the salvation of the world and the glorification of the Father.

The dialogue of Hearts between Jesus and Mary is the core of the mystical life of the Church. It is most assuredly the special portion of our contemplative life. *Cor ad cor loquitur*: as we pray the Rosary and listen to the Word in *Lectio divina,* the silent Word of the divine love takes possession of our hearts. And the Spirit, once more, is given to the World.

VII

When the Church Sings
in Honor of Mary Immaculate

WHO BETTER THAN THE CHURCH, CAN GAZE upon Mary Immaculate? Who has contemplated her more profoundly or traced her image more accurately upon the depths of her heart? On the 8th of December, a marvelous Preface sings of the beautiful Face of Mary Immaculate:

> It is truly right and just, our duty and our salvation,
> always and everywhere to give you thanks,
> Lord, holy Father, almighty and eternal God.
> For you preserved the Most Blessed Virgin Mary
> from all stain of original sin,

You wanted her to be entirely pure, intact, flawless, perfectly beautiful.

> endowed with the rich fullness of your grace,

Little and poor, You wanted her to be completely filled with Your Gift, overflowing with your abundant goodness, wholly plunged in the merciful fountain of your freely given Love.

> so that in her, you might prepare a worthy Mother for
> your Son

For only perfect purity could welcome into her womb, and then give to the world, the Son whom You beget in the unutterable purity of Your Love as Father.

and signify the beginning of the Church,
his beautiful Bride without spot or wrinkle.

For Mary is the beginning of humanity betrothed to her God Who is madly in love. She is the first flowering of mankind's beauty restored by its Savior and summoned to the eternal Marriage feast.

She, the most pure Virgin, was to bring forth a Son,
the innocent Lamb who would wipe away our offences;

For Mary Immaculate is the beginning of the costly redemption of man, she it is who provides the Victim for the sacrifice of the Cross. For Mary gives the One the Father gives, and the One who freely gives himself out of love.

you placed her above all others
to be for your people an advocate of grace
and a model of holiness.

You have made her the mirror of Your lofty purity, the privileged channel of your pure mercy: model and source, icon and fountain, humbly Immaculate and nobly Mother.

And so, in company with the choirs of Angels,
we praise you, and with joy we proclaim:

Sanctus! Sanctus! Sanctus!

About the Author

Dom Xavier Perrin OSB was born in Tours in 1958. He studied French Literature in Rennes, and the History of Art at the Sorbonne. In 1980, he entered the Abbey *Sainte Anne de Kergonan* in Brittany, where he was ordained in 1989, having studied theology at Solesmes, Fribourg, and Munich. At Ste Anne he served as guestmaster, organist, novice master, and prior, and taught dogmatic theology. He has written books and articles about the history of the Solesmes Congregation, liturgy and spirituality, and has been involved in the promotion of Gregorian chant. He was appointed Prior Administrator of the Abbey of Our Lady of Quarr on the Isle of Wight in April 2013, and elected abbot in May 2016.

His other writings include *Dom Marcel Blazy, L'ami du Roi* (Téqui, 1996), and *Dom Henri Demazure et Kergonan* (Kergonan, 2002).

Lightning Source UK Ltd.
Milton Keynes UK
UKOW04f1539181117
312914UK00001B/32/P